BE A DICK

HOW ONE PERSON CAN
CHANGE THE WORLD IN THE
MOST UNEXPECTED WAY

MARC ENSIGN

Praise for *Be a Dick*

"*One person really can make a difference, and that person can be you. In this funny and yet sometimes painfully honest account of a moment in his life, Marc Ensign tells a story about his neighbor Dick that will not only make you want to be a better human, it actually will make you a better human.*"

Hal Elrod, International Keynote Speaker and Best-selling
Author of *The Miracle Morning* and *The Miracle Equation*,
https://halelrod.com

"*This is the one time it's okay to be a Dick.*"

Wil Wheaton, Actor

"*It's rare in life to meet someone who so clearly lives what they say to do. Someone who hasn't just invented some kind 'talk' to be popular or successful. Someone where everything they do reveals the core of who they are. By highlighting one of those people — his neighbor, Dick — Marc Ensign shows you he is one of those people, too. How lucky we are that he is telling both his and Dick's stories in this gift of a book, while also showing us the path to being the very best kind of neighbor, friend, and human.*"

Tamsen Webster, Message Strategist,
https://tamsenwebster.com

"*Every now and then a book comes along that forces you to pay attention. A wonderful work of self-discovery!*"

Mark Schaefer, author of *Marketing Rebellion:
The Most Human Company Wins*,
https://businessesgrow.com

"*This book breathes life into how our lives actually look from the inside out. Marc created a brilliant storyline that gives each of us a boost in knowing that no matter where you are, that's right where you need to be. I was already a fan of his work; this just upped the game to super-fan status.*"

Bryan Kramer, Author, Business Coach,
Keynote Speaker, CEO at H2H™ Companies,
https://www.bryankramer.com

"*Once upon a time, there was a boy. He had visions of grandeur and dreams of world domination. This is not that story. This is the story of a regular guy with extraordinary self-awareness. His ability to see and communicate what is truly important in life comes through in every page of his authentic writing. Read it. Be a Dick.*"

Joel Comm, Chief Executive Shenanigator,
http://joelcomm.com

"*Anything Marc puts this much time and effort into is going to turn out to be a true masterpiece! I hope you enjoy it and apply all the insights from Dick to your own life. You are going to love the results!*"

Jairek Robbins, Owner of High Performance Ventures,
http://www.JairekRobbins.com

"*Every great story needs a hero we all want to root for — and I think the world will be rooting for Dick by the end of this book. Marc masterfully weaves narrative, self-help, and how-to to help us all make a little more sense of how to be better people in a world fraught with apocalyptic click-bait and family feuds on Facebook. This positive, uplifting story will have you laughing, crying, and ready to make positive change in the world. It's time we all grasped our inner Dick and made the world a better place. Marc can help.*"

Mike Ganino, The Mike Drop Moment Podcast,
https://www.mikeganino.com

"*In a world where information and connections are digital and in the palm of our hands, where every day, minute and moment is calendared and planned and scripted, and so much of our interactions with other humans are automated or on auto-pilot, there is an important quality of living and loving that too often gets lost.*

Being Kind.

Marc's expertly crafted stories and message remind us of the importance of being kind to one another, whether it's with someone we've known for ten years or ten minutes. We're all here on this rocky globe circling a fiery one for just a relatively short amount of time. While you're here, it's time to be a Dick."

Mike Allton, Agorapulse,
https://www.agorapulse.com

"*If you're thinking you want to change the world, start by being a Dick. That's right. I said, 'Be a Dick.' How can you be a Dick? Heck, why would you want to be a Dick? Read this book. You'll want to be a Dick, too — just like Marc Ensign. This book lays it all out for you, in a fun-to-read, easy-to-digest form, that you can actually do. Yes, you CAN be a Dick. And that's a wonderful thing.*"

Phil Gerbyshak, Vice President of Sales Training,
https://InsideSalesShow.com

"*Be kind, be helpful, be humble. There are many positive takeaways from honest and raw accounts of individual growth and enlightenment. I thoroughly enjoyed reading Be a Dick: How One Person Can Change the World in the Most Unexpected Way.*"

Scott Lesnick, Successful Business Solutions LLC,
http://www.scottlesnick.com

"*Marc's story had a following and fans long before it was ever completed. And can I just say how happy I am that Marc completed it so the rest of us could read it? It's an awesome freaking book.*"

Viveka von Rosen, Chief Visibility Officer,
http://vengreso.com

Editorial Project Management: Karen Rowe, www.karenrowe.com

Cover Design: Damonza.com

Inside Layout: Ljiljana Pavkov

Printed in the United States

ISBN: 978-1-63649-717-4 (hardcover)

ISBN: 978-1-64999-467-7 (softcover)

ISBN: 978-1-64999-468-4 (ebook)

To Aimee, Isabella, and Zachary.

For seeing me as a Dick well before this story ever happened.

(I just hope you meant it with a capital D.)

Thank you for always being there to celebrate me when I succeed and forgive me when I fail.

I love you all like crazy.

CONTENTS

BE A
DICK

FOREWORD

It was the weirdest of tweets and the craziest of responses. My then-girlfriend, Jacqueline, and I had a musical gig together. Our first time playing live in front of an audience. In rehearsal, it became clear that my idea of being a one-man-band wasn't really going to work out. So, we put out the bat signal.

I tweeted something like, "Say, anyone around Boston happen to play bass?" The idea was that I would randomly find someone who was not only a musician but who was free and might be able to pick up how to play a bunch of songs on the fly and basically perform utter magic.

Marc, who was in New York (or somewhere that wasn't Boston), replied pretty quickly that he was exactly the guy for the job. We exchanged a few emails. He said he would drive to Boston, stuff his family in a hotel room, and come play music with us. Oh, and that he was ridiculously over-qualified for the job. In short, a miracle.

And just like that, we had a bassist. Just like that, Marc did everything so far beyond what I could have expected that it felt like a dream. The audience who heard us perform figured we'd been playing together for a long time.

This was the furthest from the truth. But it all worked because of Marc's ability to slot himself right in.

In the months that followed, I saw Marc do a lot to court and romance and build a stronger network around him. He was always genuine, always working toward being helpful to others, and overall, just repeatedly succeeding at being a Dick.

You see, once you get done with this book, you're going to want to be a Dick, too. I sure do. Some would say I'm already a Dick. But I like to leave aspirations in front of me. It gives me more to attain.

Now, you? Maybe you can't play bass at a mastery level. Maybe you wouldn't abandon your family in a hotel room to run off with strangers you know solely from the Internet (for free — did I mention *free*?). But there are other ways. There are many paths to being a Dick. That's why you'll want to read this book.

Hats off to Dick and Marc, too.

Chris Brogan
Founder of the StoryLeader™ system

INTRODUCTION

"And the day came when the risk to remain tight in a bud was more painful than the risk it took to blossom."

— ANAÏS NIN

My name is Marc. And I am a Dick.

I'm a Dick to all of my friends. And to my family. I'm a Dick to people I know. And to people I don't know.

In fact, if we were to bump into each other someday, whether it be online or in real life, I would probably be a Dick to you, too.

It's nothing personal. It's just who I am. And who I believe we all should be.

But in order for any of this to make sense, we need to go back in time to New Jersey, where it all began.

(Cue Flashback Sequence)

I was only about five or six years old the first time I remember the thought passing through my mind.

I'm going to change the world.

I blame my mom for that one. She would sew two small metal snaps onto the shoulders of all of my pajamas. And then every night before going to bed, I would attach the superhero cape she made me and reenact one of several life-saving missions. This usually involved balancing on the arm of the couch while preparing to jump onto the ottoman and then the recliner in one swift motion. All in an effort to single-handedly correct the course of an entire planet while avoiding the hot lava below.

Now, there is something that happens to you as a kid when you wear a cape. I'm not talking about those cheap ones that come with the old Superman Halloween costumes. I'm talking about the cape your mom made with the first initial of your name ironed on the back.

It changes you.

To anyone looking from a distance, they would see a kid with a superhero complex and a wild imagination. But to me, that cape was a constant reminder of how my mom saw me and what I was capable of becoming. Through her eyes, I could do anything. And in my mind, that included changing the world.

This, of course, is all normal behavior for a six-year-old. Not so much for a forty-something-year-old. And yet, here we are.

You see, while I firmly believe that most kids spend their childhood dreaming of becoming a superhero or an astronaut, I also believe they eventually outgrow it and end up in dental school or someplace worse.

But not me. I didn't get the memo.

I refused to grow up into a reasonably responsible adult with a safe job, a nice house, and a family, only to disappear into the void without leaving much of a trace beyond a few plastic bottles sitting in a landfill somewhere in Nevada.

I was determined to take a different path.

As I got older, I spent the vast majority of my adolescent years sporting a pair of thick brown glasses, awkwardly curly hair, buck teeth, and braces. And on occasion, I would round out the ensemble by adding a calculator watch. That alone would have been enough to scar most kids for life. But my parents decided to kick it up a notch by moving us to a new town in the middle of third grade.

Moving to a new town is hard. Moving to a new town in the middle of the school year is really hard. Moving to a new town in the middle of the school year when you have thick brown glasses, awkwardly curly hair, buck teeth, and braces is impossible.

Yet, I walked into that classroom with a level of optimism that can only come from a kid who spent most of his life up until that point wearing a cape. I figured this move was a chance for me to start over. Maybe the kids at my new school would see through my appearance and get a glimpse of who I really was on the inside.

Spoiler alert. They didn't.

My time in high school wasn't all that much better. I mostly did my best to stay off of everyone's radar. If there was an award for "Most Likely to Be Forgotten" in the yearbook, I was the clear frontrunner. And between you and me, I was pretty okay with that because I knew I was going to be getting out of there soon enough. And that's when my life would really begin.

When I finally graduated from high school, I prepared to leave my hometown with both middle fingers displayed proudly as I left for what I assumed would be the last time. Vowing never to return. It's not that I didn't like New Jersey. I was just pretty sure that if anyone was going to make a massive difference on a global scale, they wouldn't be coming from Exit 163 off of the Garden State Parkway.

Sorry, Jon Bon Jovi.

So, with little more in my pockets than a few scattered memories, an extra pair of underwear, and a chip on my shoulder, I set out into the world to knock it off its axis.

My first stop was Boston, Massachusetts, where I attended Berklee College of Music with the goal of becoming a professional musician. You might be wondering how one chooses to change the world as a musician. And a bass player, no less.

Good question.

My original plan was to become an architect until, one afternoon, my high school jazz band went on a class trip to perform at a senior center crawling with old people. By the time we arrived, it appeared as though we were too late because everyone looked like they had already passed away. But then we started playing. And even though we weren't very good, every single person in that room got out of their wheelchairs or stepped out from behind their walkers and began to dance and clap.

Seeing the joy on their faces lit me up. And as hard as I tried, I was not able to shake that feeling. When I got home later that afternoon, I told my parents I wanted to be a musician so I could spend the rest of my life making people feel like that for a living.

So that's what I set out to do.

I spent the next few years traveling around the world with my electric bass strapped to my back. Performing in run-down little bars in Alaska. Touring through Costa Rica on a horse the size of a large dog. Visiting every state in America. Recording with Grammy Award-winning artists. And performing on Broadway in New York City.

And just in case that wasn't enough, I carved out quite a little career for myself off-stage as well. Upon seeing so many incredible musicians struggling, I came to the conclusion that I must be pretty good at marketing. If I could somehow promote myself onto a Broadway stage with no experience, perhaps I could help them do the same.

So I started my own marketing agency.

Within my first year in business, I was working with several Fortune 500 companies like Nike, American Express, and Berkshire Hathaway. At the time, my company consisted of me in a pair of sweatpants working out of a spare bedroom in my small Brooklyn apartment. Of course, I didn't want them to know this, so I took pictures of about a dozen of my friends and added them to my website with fake names and bios. And just like that, I was running a big agency.

Now, this is where things get a little fuzzy.

I woke up about ten or fifteen years later to discover that I had somehow become a reasonably responsible adult with a safe job, a nice house, and a family. Not only that, but I was living a stone's throw away from where I grew up in New Jersey.

Literally.

I mean, you could literally throw a rock out of my bedroom window, and if you didn't hit the house I grew up in, you would at least take out someone I went to high school with.

Looking at this reasonably, I understood that moving back to New Jersey didn't really mean anything.

But this was no time to be reasonable.

Having moved back home was all the proof I needed that I had failed miserably in my mission to do something meaningful with my life. In fact, I was right back where I had started with nothing significant I could point toward as proof that I had made any kind of difference in the world.

Anywhere.

I had never built a school in a third-world country. I had never walked from New York to California to raise money for a good cause. And I had never run into a burning house to save someone I didn't know.

In fact, I had never even rescued a cat from a tree. (Mostly because I'm allergic to cats and afraid of heights, but still.)

Instead, I had come home to New Jersey empty-handed with my tail neatly tucked between my legs and my mission of changing the world on life support.

I had failed. Miserably. And I knew it.

Now, don't get me wrong. There is no shortage of evidence to prove that I have achieved a level of personal and professional success of which any mother would be proud.

I'm happily married to the woman of my dreams. Together, we have two healthy children who are incredibly good people. We live in a nice house in a nice neighborhood in a nice part of the world. I'm blessed with a career that has given me the rare gift of experiencing life as a professional musician, a marketing consultant, a speaker, an author, and an entrepreneur. And that career has allowed me the opportunity to see much of the world and connect with some of the most inspiring and accomplished people in it.

Yet, there was something missing. And in my mind, it was all New Jersey's fault.

So, I did what any rational person would do at that moment. I convinced my wife and kids to sell everything we owned, abandon all of our friends and family, and move twelve hundred miles away to Tampa, Florida. Leaving behind a life I didn't really care for very much anyway.

Now, here's the thing about Florida. If you were to have asked me to make a list of all of the places where I would want to live, Florida would have been on the bottom. Right below Kalamazoo, Michigan and above Slickpoo, Idaho.

Yes, that's a real town. I looked it up.

Where I come from, Florida is considered the birthplace of all ten plagues: frogs, locusts, flies, lice, boils, hail, humidity, bad drivers, mullets, and old people. Why anyone would actually move there on purpose was beyond me.

And yet, here we are. Loading everything we have left into a moving van as we prepare for a twelve-hundred-mile journey south to a place we've never been.

It was a surreal moment. If you have ever moved what feels like halfway around the world from everyone and everything you've ever known, you have probably experienced that overwhelming feeling when the initial excitement of walking through the front door for the first time begins to wear off. It's like a punch in the face. You don't know anyone. You can't go anywhere without getting lost. And there isn't a decent slice of pizza for miles.

That feeling ultimately got the better of me while standing in our new house, staring at the mountain of boxes littering up each room.

What did I just do? I thought to myself as I looked around at the chaos.

I stole my kids away from their school. I tore my wife away from her friends. I sold most of our stuff. And I uprooted my business.

Everything that was once safe and familiar to us is now gone.

I could feel my blood pressure beginning to spike as the room started to spin.

This is it.

This is how it ends.

I was pacing back and forth, going over the events in my head, searching for the reason why I would voluntarily do this to myself and my family. Mumbling under my breath.

"What have I done? I mean, things were pretty bad, right? I know I wasn't happy. At least, I don't think I was happy. Or maybe I was. I don't even know anymore. How did I screw this up so badly? And why is it so hot around here!?"

As regret and resentment began to bubble to the surface, I found myself wishing I could get a do-over. Wishing there was a reset button I could press. Wishing that I would wake up tomorrow and things would be normal again.

But it was too late.

There was no turning back.

So, I did the next best thing.

I left.

I abandoned my wife and headed out the front door to take a walk around the neighborhood to catch my breath and talk myself off of the ledge.

But before I could escape, my wife insisted that I take the kids with me. She claimed it was for the fresh air, but I'm pretty sure it was an insurance policy to make sure I didn't start running north, never to return.

And that's when I met Dick.

BE KIND

*"I did something that made people present
their best selves to me wherever I go."*

—JIM CARREY

We were only about fifty yards from the house when we
were approached by a tall gentleman in his sixties walking
his dog, Gracie.

Now, it's important to properly set the scene here.

I was in mid-nervous breakdown. Ranting about making the biggest mistake of my life by moving to Florida.
And the last thing I needed was to bump into the old
retired guy living down the street. Especially while dragging around two whiny kids who would much rather have
gone back into the air conditioning and unpack their toys
instead of babysitting their father.

I didn't want to make a bad first impression, so I com-
posed myself long enough to get a few words out.

"How's it going?"

And then I did the "cool guy nod" while quietly praying that he would respond the way most non-psychopaths

respond: "Good. You?" And then we could both go about our business. He would finish his old man stroll around the neighborhood, and I would continue giving my kids a reason to spend the majority of their adult lives in therapy.

Only, it didn't quite happen that way.

At first, his response gave me some hope that this was going to go as expected.

"Great!"

Cool. Thanks for rubbing it in my face, by the way.

I mean, is it me, or is there nothing worse than not being great and running into someone who is great? Especially when that person is actually great.

Well, thankfully, I was going to be able to get back to my little pity party right away because…

Oh, wait. It appeared as though Mr. Look-How-Great-I-Am had more to say. Clearly, he did not realize that I was in the throes of a mental breakdown and did not have time for shenanigans.

He stopped in front of us and, without hesitation, bent down and placed his hands firmly on his knees in order to put himself at eye level with my kids.

"And who are you guys?"

Bella, who was a few weeks shy of turning ten, started by introducing herself and then transitioning seamlessly into a tirade about American Girl Dolls and her former life in New Jersey, making sure to pay homage to each of the friends she left behind.

When she ran out of things to say, her younger brother jumped in without missing a beat.

Having recently turned five, Zach spent what seemed like days talking about Legos without stopping to take a single breath. I can't say for sure, but he may or may not have described every single one of his toys in excruciating detail as well. I lost consciousness somewhere in the middle.

While all of this was happening, I took a step back and watched this complete stranger listening to my kids. And when I say "listening," I don't mean that thing adults do around children where they half pay attention and nod their head hoping for the torture to end or to put them out of their misery. I mean *really* listening. Making them feel important. Making them feel heard. Like they were the only thing in the universe that mattered at that particular moment.

And in response, these two kids were staring at this man in a way that someone might look at a glass of water after roaming the desert for weeks. They were thirsty for the attention. Desperate to be seen and to be heard.

I was so caught up in everything going on in my own little world leading up to the move that I had forgotten to check in to see how they were handling it. Listening to them unload on this poor guy made it quite clear that I had missed something.

Yet, at that moment, he kindly took on the role of the one who could make them feel whole again. By simply listening.

I was quickly jolted back to the present moment when I noticed that both kids had stopped talking. The old man straightened himself up and was now looking me in the eye with that same level of curiosity.

"My name is Dick. What's your story?"

It looked as though it was my turn.

And then, just like my kids had done, I began verbally assaulting the poor guy. I was doing my best to come across as excited and optimistic about this new direction our lives had taken, but judging by the look on his face, I was clearly falling short.

"Here. Let me help you out," he responded, letting me off the hook.

He proceeded to rattle off random details about our new neighborhood in an effort to put my mind at ease. This was all stuff I probably needed to know, but it was the furthest thing from my mind at the time.

"Garbage day is Monday and Thursday. There is a really good Chinese Food place on Route 54. The code to get through the gate is #4890."

And it didn't end there.

He pointed out each of the houses on our block with kids who were around the same age as Bella and Zach. This was to make them feel good knowing that there would be plenty of new friends around the corner. Literally and figuratively.

And to make it even easier, he suggested we stick around for the Fourth of July, which was less than a week away. Apparently, fireworks were legal in Florida, and everyone on our block came out at night to do their very best impression of the Macy's Fireworks display. Not only would it be a lot of fun, it would be a great opportunity to meet some of the other families. While blowing things up.

We talked for another ten minutes or so before I realized that my sneakers were melting to the pavement and my kids were scrounging for fallen palm tree leaves to build a shelter from the sun.

Clearly, it was time to go.

We said our goodbyes and turned around to head back toward the house. But Dick wasn't quite done.

"Wait! One more thing!" he practically shouted, since we were now about ten or fifteen feet away.

"The ceilings around here are much higher than back in New Jersey. If you want to hang anything on the walls in your house like pictures of those two kids of yours, you're probably going to need a ladder. When you do, let me know. I have two."

And then he turned around and headed home.

That last one hit me pretty hard. We didn't have a ladder. And it's true, we would probably need one at some point. But that's not why it affected me the way it did, because it had nothing to do with the ladder. It was about the open invitation that was implied by the offer.

If you need anything, I'm here. Just ask.

I couldn't imagine a better way to welcome a bunch of people who had landed in the middle of nowhere just a few hours earlier.

For the first time in what seemed like forever, I didn't feel like my world was coming to the dramatic and horrifying end I had been planning. It's not as if the source of my stress was centered around what day to drag the garbage cans out to the curb. And yet, I was at peace.

Dick could have just as easily waved and walked right past us, and I wouldn't have thought anything of it. He didn't have to listen to my kids. Or help me navigate our new neighborhood.

But he did.

For whatever reason, he made the choice to be kind to us at that moment. And that choice or that instinct or whatever it was made all the difference. I can't quite explain it other than to say that I was not the same person who had left the house forty-five minutes earlier. And the look on my wife's face when we walked back in the door confirmed that.

As I soaked up the air conditioning, I began to tell her about our little adventure.

"We were talking to the guy who lives a few houses down the street!" I told her.

"Was he nice?"

I didn't answer right away.

"The guy you met. Was he nice?"

I heard her both times. It just took me a second to answer because the word "nice" didn't quite describe him. I know a lot of people who are nice. In fact, I think most people are inherently nice. Nice is waving as you walk past someone on the sidewalk. Nice is asking how someone is doing without really paying attention to the answer. Nice is acknowledging someone else's kids without showing any interest in what they have to say.

Nice is easy.

Dick wasn't nice.

"He was kind," I responded.

She gave me a strange look. And rightfully so. It was an odd thing to say. I can't remember ever blatantly calling someone "kind" before. But I couldn't think of a better way to describe how he showed up for me and the kids in that moment.

I spent the next twenty minutes telling her all about him, as if I was seeking approval for having called him a kind person. I told her about how he had listened to the kids. And how he had given me the code to get into the development. And how he'd found a really good Chinese food place not too far away.

If the others didn't convince her, I'm pretty sure that last one got her. It had been a long day, and some dinner sounded like a really good idea. So, we decided to give it a shot and ordered from the Chinese food place Dick recommended.

It really was very good.

Afterwards, we collapsed for the rest of the night, surrounded by the remaining boxes left to be unpacked another day.

BE HELPFUL

> *"If we move one grain of sand the earth is no longer exactly the same."*

> — DAVID BOWIE

I awoke the next morning to the cries of our dog Cali wanting to go outside. I tried to put it off as long as I could, but she made my options abundantly clear. And going back to sleep was not one of them, so I got up.

Now, before we go any further, here is everything you need to know about Cali.

She is an eight-pound Bichon Frisé and Shih Tzu mix. We call that a Bicha Shit. Or at least, I do. Everyone else is pretty tired of me telling that joke. Too bad. It's a good one.

Anyway, when Cali wants something, she does this thing where she'll just stare at you and sigh.

It's weird. The dog actually sighs like she is disappointed in your life choices and is calling for a walk around the block as an intervention to help you get your act together.

And you can't say no. She's relentless.

So, I threw on my Red Sox hat, grabbed her leash, and headed out the door to explore the neighborhood together. While on our walk, we once again ran into Gracie. The same dog Dick had with him the day before. Only this time, Gracie was attached to a different human being. And whoever it was looked to be half jogging across the street, heading in our direction.

"You must be Marc! It's so great to meet you! I've heard so much about you and your lovely children! I'm Dick's wife!"

And that's when I met Rita.

Rita was maybe a foot shorter than Dick, but what she lacked in height she made up for in spunk and enthusiasm. And her energy was contagious. Especially when you consider that it was so early in the morning.

We spent the next thirty minutes or so sharing stories about family, the neighborhood, and traveling around the world. Apparently, Rita had been a flight attendant back in the day when they made fresh cookies on planes.

I didn't even know they did that.

Somewhere in our conversation, I told her about our plan to spend the day unpacking as we began the grueling task of decorating the house. It was not something I was looking forward to, and I'm pretty sure she could see it written all over my face.

Which brings me to something you should probably know before we continue.

My wife Aimee is from Queens, New York. And in just about every scenario, you will find that she is one of the most caring people to ever walk this planet. And I'm not just saying that because I assume she is going to read this eventually. It's true.

But here's the thing.

When I say, "just about every scenario," I mean that there are a few things that trigger her. And when that happens, watch out because she and her New York accent will turn on you in such a way that it would make a veteran truck driver break down in tears.

I've only seen it a few times myself. And one of those times came after questioning her ability to decorate a room in our house. It was not pretty. So, I stay quiet, and I tell her how great the plastic flowers look. Or how much I like the "1970s sitcom" orange she chose to paint the kitchen.

It's just better this way. You're going to have to trust me on this one.

The point I'm trying to make here is that we were in desperate need of some help decorating our house. But I was too scared for my life to come right out and say it. Which is why Rita could not have come into our lives at a better time. Because apparently, she had a flair for interior decorating. Or at least that's the impression I got from her because she invited me back to her home to take a tour of the house to maybe spark a few ideas, suggesting I grab Aimee along the way. That, of course, meant having to risk waking Aimee up on a Sunday morning. Another one of her triggers. However, convincing her to come with me to a stranger's house so I could trick her into looking at their stuff sounded like a challenge I was prepared to take on.

I headed back to our house and navigated the labyrinth of unpacked boxes until I made it into our bedroom.

Taking a page out of Cali's playbook, I sat on the edge of the bed and sighed until she woke up and agreed to do whatever it was I wanted her to do, as long as I would stop.

It actually worked!

Aimee got up and did her usual morning routine while I impatiently tried to move her along. We eventually headed out the door and walked the length of about seven or eight houses to Dick and Rita's, where they greeted us at the door and invited us in.

We made our way to the living room where we all sat down and did that whole "getting to know you" thing. It was an interesting dynamic to sit back and watch as Aimee gave her version of what had brought us to the neighborhood while Dick once again listened with intent. Much like he had with me and the kids.

We spent about an hour sharing stories before I cautiously commented on a picture hanging on the wall, hoping to trigger our tour without giving away my little scheme.

It worked.

Rita jumped at the chance to take us around the house, and Aimee was all too happy to join her. I wasn't quite as excited. I was prepared to lean sideways in my chair so I could see down the hall, and that would have been enough for me. But that's not what everyone else had in mind.

They were planning on the mega-tour. That included every room in the house, the garage, inside the closets, and even a secret compartment that Rita had designed and built into the house.

I'm serious.

She had a secret compartment purposely built into the house. Don't get too excited, there were just some folding chairs stashed in there. No dead bodies or anything cool.

I have to say, it was a really nice home. Tastefully decorated. Bright. With just the right number of things hanging on the wall or perched on tables and countertops. The tour had sparked many ideas for Aimee, and I could see her feverishly taking mental notes of everything she liked.

Meanwhile, I was pretty checked out of the process. I walked the tour with everyone, but I was more focused on Dick and Rita's stuff than I was on whatever feng shui they had going on. I don't mean that in a creepy "I'm going to come back and rob this place later" kind of way. It was more of an "I really don't care about any of this so… hey, that's a nice TV" kind of way.

While looking around, I noticed that one of the rooms had a bunch of Emmy Awards sitting on a shelf in the corner.

Or at least I think it was a bunch. I don't know what you would normally call a lot of Emmys congregating on one shelf together. Is it a flock of Emmys, maybe? A herd? A swarm? I'm not sure. It just seemed like a lot, is what I'm getting at.

And for the record, they weren't fake. These were the real deal. As in, "I would like to thank Jesus, the Academy, and my parents for making this possible" type of Emmys.

I was pretty shocked. It's not something you see every day. And yet, we all just walked past them as if they weren't there and made our way into a closet in a nearby room. They were never mentioned by anyone the entire time. In fact, I don't think Aimee even saw them because they were pretty tucked away.

By the time our tour was over, Dick and Rita came clean. Apparently, they had worked with an interior decorator on several of the rooms, which made us feel better about our lack of decorating prowess. However, we were still starving for any help they could offer.

Rita gave Aimee some pointers while telling her about a few of the stores where she shopped for the kind of stuff we liked. You could see by the look in Aimee's eyes that our plans for the afternoon now involved shopping.

Meanwhile, Dick was busy looking for a pen and paper because he wanted to write down my email address. It seemed like an odd request. However, he had a reason. Over the years, he had accumulated a list of some of the best landscapers, plumbers, electricians, and pool companies in the area and wanted to send it over to me. It was good timing, too. We had already gotten a letter in our mailbox about the overgrown palm trees on our property needing to be trimmed.

We said our goodbyes and headed back toward our house. The whole way, Aimee was talking through some of her new ideas while I nodded agreeably, still a little nervous about the plastic flower incident I mentioned earlier. I'm telling you, it was a difficult time in our lives.

Back at the house, we finished unpacking before heading to a few of the stores Dick and Rita had suggested.

For the record, I'm not really one for shopping. Especially for household goods. However, it wasn't as bad as I would have thought. Perhaps because we had more direction than normal.

We ended up getting a bunch of stuff. Mostly decorations for the main living areas. Stuff we probably never would have gotten if Dick and Rita had not walked us through their house.

As we began to unbox everything and set it up, something interesting happened. Our new house began to feel more and more like our new home.

That's the thing about being helpful. It doesn't take much to make a big impact on someone else.

We had one more bag to go through and then we were done decorating for the night. Inside was a big picture frame that Aimee really liked. She circled the living room a few times before finding the perfect spot on the wall.

Pausing for a second, she turned around and looked at me while still holding onto the frame.

"Do we have a ladder?"

BE HUMBLE

"We are all apprentices in a craft where no one ever becomes a master."

—ERNEST HEMINGWAY

It had been a week or two since the move, and things were beginning to normalize. However, something was still bugging me, and I needed to get to the bottom of it. But in order to do so, I was going to have to catch Dick while out on a walk so I could talk to him privately.

Now, before you read this next part, I want to be clear that I was not stalking him. This is perfectly normal behavior. Sort of. Okay, fine. I was stalking him a little. But I was stalking him in the nicest way possible. There is such a thing, you know.

We have a big window in front of the house, which makes it nearly impossible for someone to pass by outside without Cali barking as if she is protecting us from the apocalypse. On most occasions, this is incredibly annoying. However, if you are trying to catch up with your neighbor as he passes by your house, it can come in handy.

Every time she barked, I would peek out the window to see who it was. Most of the time, it was a car or a kid on a bike, but every so often, Cali would go "super red alert" and start breathing fire, which usually meant there was another dog.

And that was my cue.

Because if there was another dog, there was a pretty good chance that it would be Gracie, and that meant Dick would likely be following right behind her. At that point, all I would have to do is grab Cali and her leash and — "ta-da," I bump into him.

It was a pretty good plan if I do say so myself.

Sometime that afternoon, I was working in my office down the hall within earshot of the front door, waiting for the signal. And sure enough, like clockwork, Cali lost her mind over something walking past the house.

Guess who?

I went to grab the leash, but as soon as I did, Cali gave me the stink-eye. She had just been out an hour earlier and was not terribly enthusiastic over the idea of taking another trip around the block. She can be a tough nego- tiator, so I promised her some peanut butter on a spoon when we got back. And with that, she became a little more agreeable, provided that it was a quick run without all of the idle chitchat. I agreed to the terms and put on her leash, and we headed out the door.

I waved over to Dick as I tried to act surprised at the coincidence of us both being out for a walk at the same time. I quickly opened with a comment about the weather in an effort to distract him from realizing that I had an agenda beyond being outside to walk my dog. I'm a pretty bad actor, so I'm sure he wasn't buying it. Instead of carrying on with the charade, I came right out and hit him with it.

"Hey… so… ummm… what's up with the Emmys?"

Yup. I went there.

Oh c'mon, you know you were thinking it, too. Don't start acting like I'm the only nosey one around here. In fact, I bet you did a Google search for "Emmy winners named Dick" while reading that last chapter, didn't you? I thought so. And for the record, it's not Dick Cavett or Dick Van Dyke. Nice try, though.

Anyway, it was a valid question.

I didn't know much about the Emmys. But I did know that they don't just give those things away to every Tom, Dick, and Harry. So, where had they come from? And while we're on the subject, what kind of nutjob has a bunch of Emmys sitting on a shelf in the corner of a room in their house and isn't telling everyone they know about them at least three times a day?

Look at me, for example.

I watched the Emmys once a few years ago and I must have tweeted about it for the next week and a half. In fact, I still won't shut up about it right now as I write this book. So, I can only imagine what I would have done with a bunch of them stacked up in the corner of a room in my house. At the very least, I would have turned a few of them into a pair of earrings or had one of them tattooed on my face.

Alright, maybe not the tattoo, but I will say without hesitation that if I had won a few Emmys, you would know about it.

Every. Freaking. Day.

And yet, Dick never mentioned it. Not once.

I've been to his house. I've walked around the block with him. I've met his wife. I've even seen his super-secret hideaway where he stashes all his folding chairs.

Nothing.

Well, now it's out there. And we're going to figure this thing out one way or another.

I stopped talking while anxiously waiting to hear what he had to say. At this point, I was pretty sure Jason Bourne was involved, and somehow Dick had saved Mary Tyler Moore from the Russian mafia. And as a token of her appreciation, she had given him her Emmys. Looking back now, it seems a little far-fetched. However, it could have happened! You never know!

We walked in silence for a minute or two as I began to get physically ill over my concern for the well-being of Mary Tyler Moore. And then he finally responded.

"It's just something I do."

Yup. Got it. And?

Wait. Is that all you're going to say? Just something you do? Who answers a question like that?! Training your body to wake up and get out of bed exactly fifteen minutes before your spouse so you don't have to be the one who has to make the bed is just "something you do."

Not that I do that.

Okay. So, I totally do that. But in my defense, whenever I make the bed, Aimee waits until I leave the room before redoing it anyway, so why should I even bother?

Regardless. What's important here is what's behind that answer.

"It's just something I do."

We pretty much left it at that as we turned the final corner in our trip around the block and he headed back toward his house.

Now it was killing me. This was actually even worse. My mind was racing with ideas. I'm pretty sure at one point I was convinced he had stolen them from the Academy and was now on the run from the red carpet police. If there even is such a thing.

It took a little while to unpack it, but the more I thought about it, the more I began to understand.

It wasn't a big deal. Not in the grand scheme of things, anyway. Don't get me wrong. I'm sure they meant something to him. I'm sure he was proud of his accomplishments. I'm sure there were days when he took a step back and had to pinch himself.

However, there was no need for outside validation. He didn't have an Instagram account dedicated to them; he didn't use them as his profile picture on LinkedIn; he didn't post "Exhausted from polishing all my Emmy's again today! #Blessed!" on Facebook.

And he didn't make them into a pair of earrings or have them tattooed on his face.

Because it was just something he did. They were never meant to define who he was.

Or at least that's how I chose to see it. I didn't have much of a choice. It was another week or so before he actually told me the real story while we were digging through an old box of his pictures.

As it turned out, Dick had spent the better part of thirty or forty years as a producer and director for some of the biggest sporting events on network television. Apparently, he was a pretty big deal. If you have a specific game etched in your memory from your childhood, there's a good chance that Dick was there.

And as a result of his work and the work of his team, they had won a bunch of Emmys. And by the looks of all of the pictures in the box, they were well deserved. Because one picture after another captured a significant moment in sports history. And there was Dick. Right in the middle of it all.

Yet, it was just something he did.

We must have spent hours going through those pictures as he told me many of the stories that accompanied them. You could see the pride radiating from his face. As if he was experiencing each story again for the first time.

At one point, he stopped and put the pictures away as we sat there talking, and he turned the tables on me.

"So, what's it like to perform on Broadway?"

And that's when I got it.

It took every ounce of strength I had not to tell him every excruciating detail of my life as a professional musician. Because at that point in my life, my accomplishments defined me. I had blurred the line between who I was and what I did. And I'd never realized how unhealthy that was until that moment.

So instead, I paused for a few seconds and smiled.

"It's just something I do."

And we just left it at that.

BE COMPASSIONATE

"If you want others to be happy, practice compassion. If you want to be happy, practice compassion."

—DALAI LAMA XIV

Later that week, Dick invited me, Aimee and the kids out for ice cream.

Actually, let me rephrase that. It wasn't so much that he invited us as he wouldn't stop talking about the fact that this one particular ice cream shop in town had the best coffee chocolate chip ice cream on the planet and insisted we try it.

Now, between you and me, I'm not a big fan of coffee chocolate chip ice cream. It's probably my least favorite of the chocolate chip family of flavors. However, I agreed to take one for the team and give it a shot. Besides, Dick had it in his head that this place was going to put coffee chocolate chip on the map for me, and I'm pretty sure he wasn't going to let it go until we tried it.

I grabbed Aimee and the kids, and the four of us headed down the street to Dick and Rita's house.

We rang the doorbell, thinking that they would come right out and we would head over together, but Rita wasn't quite ready, so Dick invited us in while we waited.

As we stood in the foyer of their house, I caught something I hadn't noticed on our first visit a few weeks earlier. We were surrounded in every direction by something incredibly fragile. On the left was a giant mirror. On the right was a ceramic bowl. In front of us was a glass picture frame. And I'm pretty sure the rest of the house was made from a combination of butterfly wings and Fabergé eggs.

Or at least that's how it looked from the perspective of the parent of a five-year-old-boy.

Except that Zach wasn't any ordinary five-year-old boy. If there is anything that kid excels at, it is the ability to break just about anything within a fifty-foot radius. And in some cases, without even touching anything. I love that kid, but let me tell you, he is the human equivalent of an EF5 tornado.

Now, you're probably thinking that I am exaggerating in an effort to make a point, and in most cases, I would probably agree with you. But this is not one of those cases.

Allow me to give you an example of what we're dealing with, and then you can decide.

Every summer while living in New Jersey, we would take a weekend trip to Hershey's Chocolate World in Pennsylvania. For those of you who have never been there, it's an amusement park where the old Hershey's Chocolate Factory used to be. Imagine eating your weight in chocolate in the middle of the summer right before going on a roller coaster ride and then trying your best not to throw it all up. That's pretty much what we're talking about.

One year, we were in the gift shop and I was put in charge of Zach, who was only three years old at the time. Since Zach was belted into his stroller, Aimee was fairly confident that she could leave the two of us alone for a few minutes without incident.

Aimee was wrong.

While I was walking down one of the aisles in the store, Zach reached out and snatched the first thing his hand came in contact with, an oversized Reese's Peanut Butter Cup mug. Before I realized what was happening, he dropped it on the ground and watched with glee as it shattered on impact.

The rest of what you are about to read all happened in slow motion.

Zach grabbed a second mug, which instantly suffered a similar demise. At this point, I had one choice. Make a break for it and get him out of this aisle. The only thing standing in my way, aside from the broken glass on the floor, was what seemed like miles and miles of oversized coffee mugs.

I started to move. Quickly at first, but then Zach stuck out his hand and swiped three more mugs off the shelf and onto the floor. He grabbed another, at which point I attempted to take it from him and accidentally knocked it out of his hand.

Everyone in the store looked on in horror as this continued until we made it to the end of the aisle before turning around to see what was left in our wake. It looked like a warzone. The carnage on the ground consisted of nine mugs. Or about three hundred dollars.

One of the teenage girls working the floor came up to us as we stood in silence. We all stared down the aisle, wondering who was going to speak first. I imagine the employee handbook frowns upon kicking customers in the teeth. Otherwise, I'm pretty sure that would have been the appropriate reaction. As politely as possible, given the circumstances, she suggested we leave the store. And we were all too happy to oblige.

While making our way toward the exit, we passed Aimee, who was standing near the cashier with Bella. She was staring in the direction of the commotion with a look of absolute horror on her face.

"Was that Zach?"

There was a little glimmer of hope, but I'm pretty sure she knew the answer before she ever asked the question.

I didn't respond. I didn't have to.

"Oh."

And then she returned to her conversation with the cashier, pretending not to know us.

And now that same kid was standing in the foyer of my new neighbor's house, where everything was starting to look like an oversized Reese's Peanut Butter mug.

Zach's focus locked in on a large ceramic bowl sitting innocently on the table by the door as he started to walk as if being pulled towards it. Without hesitation, Aimee and I joined forces in what can only be described as something out of an old Wonder Twins cartoon. She turned into a majestic bird ready to snatch him away from the bowl and I turned into a useless puddle of water.

High-five to all of my fellow Generation Xers. As for the rest of you, I'll give you a minute to look up the Wonder Twins so you understand the joke.

We got between Zach and the bowl and did what I firmly believe most parents would have done in that situation.

We whisper-yelled.

That's an actual thing. I looked it up. It's when you clench your teeth really tightly and scrunch up your face as if you just ate a lemon and proceed to aggressively whisper at someone without moving your lips.

"ZACHARY! Put your hands in your pockets and don't touch anything! Don't even touch the floor. Suspend yourself in mid-air right here and we will come get you when we are ready to leave!"

And that's when Dick jumped in.

"I'm sure he's fine."

Dick bent down and got to eye-level with him again. Just like on the day we'd met.

"We're buddies, right?"

Zach quietly nodded his head in agreement.

"Okay. Well, since we're buddies, you wouldn't want to break anything of mine, would you?"

This time, Zach quietly shook his head no.

"Great! Thank you, Zach! You can go take a look. Just be careful."

And that was it.

Dick didn't see the kid who had rid the world of an entire set of oversized coffee mugs. He was able to step outside of himself, and as a result, he was able to see a kid who was in a stranger's home where there was no one else his age and no toys to play with. A kid who just wanted to go out for some ice cream. A kid who was reprimanded in front of everyone for doing nothing wrong.

Whatever it would have cost to replace the bowl or the picture frame had he broken it was a fraction of what it was worth for this little five-year-old boy to feel welcome in this man's house.

It's difficult to put our own emotions aside long enough to see the world through a different set of eyes. To step into the proverbial shoes of someone or something else in order to truly understand what might be motivating them. To feel what they feel. Even if just for a minute.

We've all been in that situation where we weren't getting what we needed from a grumpy waitress or rude driver. So, we jump to conclusions. Pass judgment on who we believe them to be. Define their entire existence by this one short-lived experience that we have shared with them.

But rarely do we take a moment to consider that there might be more to the story than what we have physically witnessed. That perhaps they are having a horrible day. Maybe they were just yelled at by their boss. Or they got in a fight with their spouse. Maybe their child is home sick. Or maybe they are at the end of their third shift and the last ounce of energy they have is being used to keep them on their feet.

Or maybe they just want some ice cream.

And when seen from a place of compassion, Zach acted differently. The bowl survived. As did everything else in the house. Not because we forced him to stay put. But because we let him go.

At that moment, Rita turned the corner with a big smile on her face, ready to get some ice cream. One by one, we all headed out the door in order to see if this coffee chocolate chip really was everything Dick said it was going to be.

It was good. But it didn't change my mind about coffee chocolate chip ice cream. Just don't tell Dick I said that.

BE THOUGHTFUL

"To the world you may be one person, but to one person you may be the world."

—DR. SUESS

Over the course of the next month, I saw Dick on a pretty regular basis. Mostly, while we were both out walking our dogs. But on occasion, we would go out to dinner or order a pizza and watch a movie. One of my not-so-proud moments included falling asleep on his couch while watching *Silver Linings Playbook*. I still haven't seen the ending, so don't spoil it for me.

At this point, it had been about two months since we'd moved to Florida, and we had begun to settle in. The kids had made a bunch of new friends in our neighborhood just like Dick had promised they would during our first conversation together. Aimee was teaching at an elementary school not far from where we lived. And I was busy working from home in my office, running my marketing agency.

Life was moving right along as you would expect.

And then, one afternoon while everyone was either at work or at school, the doorbell rang.

It was Dick.

I hadn't seen him for what felt like a week, which was a little out of the ordinary. I was also surprised to see him because it wasn't like him to come by unannounced, so there had to be a reason for it. As I opened the door, he took a few steps into the house and began to explain his reason for stopping by.

"I can't stay. I just wanted to drop in for a minute because I have something for you."

Part of me was hoping that I had won the Publisher's Clearing House Sweepstakes. But I didn't see a giant check or balloons. And I'm pretty sure Ed McMahon is no longer with us, and since that was his thing, it wasn't looking too good.

Bummer.

I noticed that Dick had one hand awkwardly hiding behind his back. But before I could ask him about it, he got into the reason why he'd stopped by.

"I heard your birthday was coming up, and I wanted to do a little something for you, seeing that you are celebrating away from all of your friends and family this year."

I had to think about that for a second.

He was right. It had never actually occurred to me until he said something. I didn't have anyone to celebrate my birthday with. Except for Aimee and the kids, of course. But they didn't really count because they have to celebrate with me whether they liked it or not.

At this point, it became quite clear that he was hiding some kind of gift behind his back. Knowing that this whole setup was leading to a present made me nervous. Normally, when there is some long-winded disclaimer that precedes a gift, it usually ends in some kind of ugly sweater vest that I have to pretend to be excited about and wear around the neighborhood.

But there was no ugly sweater vest this time. Instead, he handed me a plastic bag.

Now, before we get into what was actually in the plastic bag, I feel obligated to set the record straight. When two men exchange a gift, a plastic bag is a perfectly acceptable form of gift wrap. Other acceptable forms include newspaper, tin foil, and the bag the gift actually came in. I just don't want you to get all judgmental about it. The bag was fine.

I looked at the plastic bag, and inside was a baseball.

It was an odd choice for a gift. I supposed I should lay off wearing the Red Sox hat for a bit if he was giving me a baseball for my birthday. I mean, I like baseball and everything. I just was not really sure I needed one.

Dick saw the puzzled look on my face, pointed at the ball, and said, "Take a closer look."

I looked back down and noticed some writing on the ball. They looked like signatures. I twisted the ball around a few times until I caught a name I recognized and stopped.

Nomar Garciaparra.

He is the retired Hall of Fame shortstop for the Boston Red Sox.

When Dick saw I was catching on to what he had just given me, he began to fill me in on the details.

"I just got back from Pennsylvania after assisting for the past week with the Little League World Series," he began. "While I was there, I searched for any retired Red Sox players who were attending the game or working in the booth so I could get them to sign this baseball for you as a birthday gift."

I was speechless.

And then, one by one he told me the story behind each of the names on the ball. Including the producer who'd found the ball in the booth and had taken it upon himself to sign it even though he had never played baseball, let alone for the Boston Red Sox.

I was still speechless. Although I did find it kind of funny that a producer had crashed Dick's idea and signed the ball when he wasn't looking.

When he was done, he wished me a happy birthday and turned to leave. I thanked him awkwardly and said goodbye as I closed the door behind him.

He was gone.

I was a bit relieved because I didn't want him to see that I was on the verge of tears as I held this stupid baseball covered in signatures I could barely read. I had never received a gift like this before. From anyone.

Don't get me wrong. I have been given my share of pretty amazing gifts from friends and family before. I don't want to discount that. And I certainly don't want to discourage them from continuing to lavish me with presents.

But this was different.

The amount of thought that had gone into handing me this autographed baseball was significant. Forget all the logistics involved like being at the game, buying a baseball, and then finding people to sign it. That stuff is difficult to pull off, but not impossible. The part that got me was that he had been away from home. And he had thought of me. And that my birthday was coming up. And that I was far away from my friends and family. And that I might not have anyone to celebrate with.

A flood of emotion hit me as I stood in front of the closed door with a single thought swirling around in my head.

This is who I want to be.

I didn't say it out loud. Or at least I don't think I did. And if I did, nobody was home except for Cali, and she knows I talk to myself all of the time, so she wouldn't have thought anything of it.

I was just so overwhelmed by the gesture.

Do you know how there is always someone who says, "It's the thought that counts" every time you receive a gift? Well, apparently, it is true. It really is the thought that counts. Because this gift cost nothing and yet it was probably the most thoughtful gift I had ever received.

It reminded me of that feeling I'd gotten back in school when I had performed at the senior center with the high school jazz band. Life had gotten in the way since then, and I had forgotten about the day I'd run home from the senior center and made that grand statement to spend the rest of my life making people feel joy like that as I jumped head first into a career as a musician.

And now here we are, years later, and I'm on the receiving end of that same type of gesture, getting to see first-hand what it was like.

This is who I want to be.

There it was again. Repeating over and over again in my head. Like it was teasing me. Challenging me to dig deeper.

I wasn't quite sure what to do with it yet, but I knew there was a lot to unpack. Something I'm not usually very good at when I'm distracted by the chaos around the house. Even when I'm the only one home.

So, I walked into my office and placed the baseball on my desk and decided to take a few hours off. I headed down the hall toward the door leading into the garage where I stored my bike.

Thinking that perhaps some fresh air would help me get some clarity.

BE GENEROUS

"I've learned that you shouldn't go through
life with a catcher's mitt on both hands.
You need to be able to throw something back."

— MAYA ANGELOU

For those of you who don't know me, I'm an avid cyclist. Spending a few hours on my bike is my favorite choice of escape. It's where I go to clear my head and get away from the rest of the world for a little bit. Not to mention, it's a chance to fulfill my lifelong dream of wearing Spandex in public without people pointing and laughing at me.

If there was ever a time when I needed a little bit of clarity, this was it. So, I jumped on my bike and headed out of the neighborhood as all of these thoughts ran through my head.

I know I'm probably coming across a little overdramatic with the whole "this is who I want to be" thing. It makes me cringe a little as I write about it. I mean, Dick didn't split the atom. Or cure cancer. And, last time I checked, there were still children starving all over the world. But I think that's what made everything he had done up to that point so extraordinary. Dick was just being himself.

And that's the type of person I want to be.

Someone who is able to make a difference in the world just by being themselves. I felt like this was what I had been searching for since the first time I'd taken that leap off the arm of the couch in my little snap-on cape.

I thought back to the day we'd moved to the neighborhood and I'd bumped into Dick on the street for the first time with Bella and Zach. And ran through each interaction after that. Remembering the little details that made it stand out to me. Trying to figure out what it all meant.

I wish I could tell you that I was a mile or two in before I had this big "aha" moment that led to uncovering the meaning of life. But it didn't quite work out that way.

In fact, I was about twenty miles into my ride when I turned the corner back into our development as I headed toward my house, no clearer than I had been when I'd left an hour and a half earlier.

As I passed Dick's house, I found myself hoping he would be outside, or taking a walk, or watering the lawn. Maybe he would say something that would trigger a profound thought that would give me more clarity, as he has done in the past.

But he wasn't home. And he wasn't outside either.

Maybe I'm overthinking this whole thing. I had this unshakable desire to want to be like Dick and make a difference in someone else's life. Just like he had done with mine.

Maybe the first step in doing that is simply sharing my story.

As a marketer with an incredibly unsuccessful blog about internet marketing, it was a great story to share with the one steady reader I had. Me. But more than that, there was something about this man that was worth sharing, and it felt greedy to keep it all to myself.

So, I got back to the house and ran into my office and locked the door behind me. I positioned the baseball on my desk so I could see it out of the corner of my eye as a reminder of what I was about to write and why I was about to write it.

I opened a new document and sat there for a minute as that blank page stared back. Daring me to write something on it. And then, across the top of the page, I began to type.

From Now On I'm Going to Be a Dick to Everyone I Meet Online

What followed that title was a 1,355-word manifesto encouraging those who read it to be kinder. And more helpful. And more humble. And more compassionate. It was a promise to myself and a challenge to the world to show up to life differently. To be a better human being.

When I was done, I proudly stepped back to take one last look at what I had written before I published it on my blog, took a shower, and went to bed.[1]

When I woke up the next morning, I checked my email and found that someone had left a comment. Actually, there was more than one. In total, it looked as though

---

[1] https://marcensign.com/dick

there were maybe twenty comments. That may or may not sound like a lot to you, but up until that point, the highest number of comments I had ever gotten on one of my blog posts was zero. And this was a lot more than zero.

> *What a wonderful post! I'm going to encourage everyone I know to read this and to become a Dick.*

> *This post reminds me of who I want to be online, and I thank you for the nudge to be who I should be.*

> *This post just made me a fan! I'll be endeavoring to be more of a "Dick" in the future.*

> *Thank you for these inspiring words. They refreshed and clarified my intention to be a Dick to everyone I meet.*

Dick had gone viral.

And while that may be a bad thing when it comes to your anatomy, for a blog post, it's the ultimate goal. My only question was how it had taken off so quickly. So, I jumped on social media and started poking around.

And that's when I found it.

There were hundreds of people mentioning me and linking to the post on Twitter. And they all stemmed from one very unlikely source.

Wil Wheaton.

If you don't know Wil Wheaton, he is the actor who, as a child, played Gordie in the movie *Stand by Me*.

Of course, he's done a bunch of other impressive stuff since, but none of it seemed as random as the kid from *Stand By Me*. So, that's the one I chose to use for the book. Sorry, *Star Trek* fans.

Somehow, someone had shared the post with Wil Wheaton, who in turn had shared it on Twitter.

This is the one time it's okay to be a Dick.

Apparently, he has a pretty significant platform, and he uses it to spread positivity online in his own special way. By encouraging people NOT to be a dick.

Notice the lowercase "d."

So, when he saw my post, it happened to play off of the tagline he often uses. That was enough to have him share it with his two million followers.

Now, you're probably wondering how he shared this post with two million people and only twenty people commented. Good question. When tens of thousands of people try to visit your website at the exact same moment, your website will sometimes shut down.

And that's what happened.

Three times.

Luckily, one of the people who was able to read the post before my website crashed was a server technician, and he saw an opportunity to help. He reached out and asked if I would be willing to share my login information so he could go in and fix it. I don't recommend ever sending your passwords to a complete stranger. But, I sent my passwords to a complete stranger. What choice did I have? Within an hour or two, my server was up and running, and it hasn't gone down since.

I thanked him profusely and offered to pay for being so generous with his time, and he simply responded, "Don't worry about it. I'm happy to be a Dick."

That was the moment I realized that I had stumbled upon something special. This wasn't a message. This was a movement.

Over the next week or so, hundreds of thousands of people read that post. I had thousands of people share it across all social media platforms. I received hundreds of comments. And my inbox was filled with email after email from grateful readers who wanted to share their story of someone who was a Dick in their life.

I was in awe. And I rode that wave for the better part of two or three weeks.

Eventually, the dust began to settle, and just like everything that blows up on the internet, people moved on to the next shiny penny. This was no different.

It was one of those "don't cry because it's over, smile because it happened" moments. What I didn't realize was that this was just the beginning.

BE AUTHENTIC

> *"In most of our human relationships, we*
> *spend much of our time reassuring each other*
> *that our costumes of identity are on straight."*
>
> — RAM DASS

While that post about Dick was my first taste of internet fame, my second was only a few weeks later. But it didn't go quite as well.

As I said earlier, I had a very unsuccessful blog. And the posts that I wrote over the next few weeks proved that fact. Inching me closer and closer to one-hit-wonder status and being forever known as the Dexys Midnight Runners of the blogging world.

I was digging pretty deep for another hit when I remembered something that had happened a few years earlier while I was still living in New Jersey.

I was at a local networking event rubbing elbows with some of New Jersey's finest business owners when a guy walked into the room in a hurry, stuffed a business card in everyone's face, and then left. It wasn't the first time I had fallen victim to the hit-and-run of a bad networker. But as I was about to find out, there was something special about this one.

A few days after my initial encounter with him, I received a follow-up email. You could tell that it was not personal by the fact that everyone he'd met that night was copied on it. And normally, I would have ignored it and moved on. Except that the opening of the email made it nearly impossible to stop reading.

> *Sorry about this mass email, but it's more*
> *efficient on my end. I'm also kind of a "semi-*
> *professional networker" with 10,000 people in*
> *my Gmail contacts list, 1,000 friends on my*
> *various Facebook accounts (even though I don't*
> *use Facebook myself), 1,000 followers on Twitter,*
> *and Google will "auto-populate" my name, so*
> *perhaps some of you "beginning" networkers*
> *will learn some tips of how I'm always trying to*
> *create a "win-win" (this skill set was stressed a lot*
> *when I got my MBA from NYU).*

You had me at hello.

And the rest of the email just kept getting better. Apparently, the main reason he attended networking events was because he was in search of a wife.

I had to read that a few times too, so if you need to take a pause, I understand.

He proceeded to describe his ideal woman in excruciating detail. Age, education, preferred size, travel experience, religion, and more.

Had the letter ended there, it would have been enough to have been considered mildly inappropriate but hardly offensive. Good for him for being clear on what he was looking for in a mate, I suppose.

It's what followed next that kicked the whole thing up a notch.

It was a fee schedule. Or I guess you should call it a reward schedule.

If you were to successfully set him up on a date, you would get $100 cash. The second date was $200. All the way up to the fifth date with a variety of incentives along the way.

It became increasingly difficult not to be horrified as I got deeper into the letter.

I stuffed the email in a folder on my computer and completely forgot about it until a year or two later, when I was attempting to come up with a new topic for my blog. After much consideration, I decided that it was time to drag it out of the vault. What I ended up with was a post about the *dos and don'ts* of networking and building relationships. This email was merely used as a really solid example of what *not* to do.

I was careful to strip away anything that could potentially identify the author of the email. Mostly to protect his identity but also because the point of the post wasn't really about him. Truth be told, it wasn't my best work, but it was a pretty good post. There was a decent lesson in there if you were willing to look past the sheer absurdity of it all.

It didn't take long for the post to start grabbing attention. I guess I had hit a nerve. Again.

By the end of the first day, it had been written about on several different sites, including the Huffington Post, which caused a huge spike in traffic.

Welcome to going viral. Population: me.

By the time I awoke the next morning, a small mob of about 400 readers had formed within the comments section of the post. All of them condemning and diagnosing this guy. Cursing him and his family. And even accusing me of making the entire thing up.

Deep down inside, I knew it was getting ugly, but I couldn't tear my attention away from all of the traffic it was generating.

And it wasn't just traffic. I was receiving calls from *The Steve Harvey Show* to appear as a guest, *The New York Post* to be interviewed for the paper, and a host of other radio shows, podcasts, blogs, TV shows, and websites. I found myself in the car, listening to the local morning show on the radio as they were talking about it. I found an article in a Belgian newspaper that wrote the story as if *I* had been the one in search of a wife. And it even made its way onto Howard Stern.

It had gotten completely out of hand.

By the third day, I was well on my way to breaking two million visitors to the post when I happened to take a stroll through the comments section and was horrified by what I saw.

He had been outed.

During the night, a commenter had confirmed that the story was true. And he knew it was true because he had gone on a job interview and had been handed a piece of paper with this exact same wish list.

Now there were bigger problems.

As further proof, the comment included the name, address, and phone number of the guy who originally wrote the letter. And by the time I saw it, it was too late. People had discovered similar posts he had left on Craigslist and articles on other sites.

They had found their man. And they wanted his head on a platter.

The mob that I had unwittingly created began to reach out to him. They tracked down his Facebook page, Twitter account, email, office address, and home phone number in order to make sure he was aware of what a scumbag the world thought he was.

And my post led the mob right to him.

Deep down inside, I knew this was not what I wanted to be known for.

I couldn't be the guy who approached life in this extraordinary way on the one hand while tearing down another human being on the other. Had I learned nothing?

I needed to make a choice. Was I a Dick, or was I a dick?

Once I stepped back and took an honest look, it was an easy decision. I took the post down and replaced it with a short letter explaining my predicament.[2]

> *Don't tell me, let me guess. This isn't the post you were looking for, right?*
>
> *Sorry. I took it down.*
>
> *You are probably thinking that it is because of some ugly letter I got from an attorney. It's not. At least not yet anyway. That may change.*

---

[2] https://marcensign.com/sorry

The reason I took it down was because the point of my post had been missed and was replaced with a "grab your pitchfork and torch and let's kill the monster" style response. And I want no part of that.

My purpose is to spread my message to as many people as possible. But not this way. And not this message.

I wrote a post a few weeks ago entitled "From Now on I'm Going to Be a Dick to Everyone I Meet Online" about my neighbor Dick. A warm and welcoming guy. The ambassador of my new neighborhood. And I talked about how I strive to be that person online. To everyone.

And that means everyone.

Keeping this post up doesn't allow me to be a Dick. Just a dick.

So, rather than being disappointed that you aren't able to see the car accident from where you are sitting, I would ask that you read the other post instead. That is the message I want to share with the world. Not the one that you expected to find here.

I hope you can understand.

The next morning, I awoke to an angry mob. And they had turned their attention on me. I was accused of creating a bait and switch. It was recommended that I crawl in a hole and die. And someone actually called me a doofus.

I kind of enjoyed that last one.

But then a funny thing happened. Once the angry mob got tired and decided to focus their attention on someone else, the tone changed.

> *Someone sent me a link to this page, and I must say... you've just made my day. I think I'll spend the rest of my day actively being a Dick as well.*

> *I'm proud of you, and I give you large amounts of kudos for being an amazingly decent human being. You're a rare species, sir, and I give you my respect for it.*

> *Beautiful! I want to be a Dick to everyone online, too! EVERYONE! Thanks for the inspiration!*

And they kept coming.

Looking back, I lost a lot of opportunities by taking the post down. I mean, I could have been on *The Steve Harvey Show*! But that wouldn't have been authentic to who I really was deep down inside.

I've had a lot of good days and a lot of bad days since, but taking that post down was a decision I never regretted.

And since then, I have not written a single word that wasn't true to who I am. Inside and out.

BE PRESENT

> *"To live is the rarest thing in the world.*
> *Most people just exist."*
>
> —OSCAR WILDE

All of this attention I was getting online was resulting in valuable new friendships and opportunities I probably would not have enjoyed otherwise. And as a result of a few of those relationships, I was being asked to speak at industry-related conferences more than usual. One time, in particular, was a social media event in Halifax.

That's in Canada, for you non-world travelers out there.

So, here's the cool thing about speaking in Canada. It meant that I was now an international speaker. And you know that that means, don't you? I could double my fees!

Unfortunately, I wasn't getting paid to speak, and last I checked, two times zero was still zero.

You see, short of a few local workshops, I wasn't doing much speaking. I dreamed about what it would be like to take the stage at one of those big industry conferences. But it wasn't something I was actively chasing.

And then I got the call to speak in Halifax, and that's where I got the bug.

One of the main reasons I was so excited about speaking at this particular event was because I desperately wanted to be one of the cool kids, and many well-known influencers like Gary Vaynerchuk and Scott Stratten were going to be there. Now, if you don't recognize either of those names, don't feel too bad about it. They are both pretty big in the marketing world.

My plan was to milk this thing for all it was worth. And that's what I did.

The title of my talk was *Search Engine Humanization*. It was my spin on search engine optimization, which is the method of getting websites to rank on search engines like Google and… well, Google. It's not like people are using Yahoo! anymore.

This was the first time I publicly introduced many of the principles I had learned from Dick. Only, it was neatly wrapped in a nice little package for my fellow marketing geeks. In fact, there was no mention of Dick anywhere in the talk. Just the lessons.

The talk went really well. I got a lot of great feedback. A few people even laughed at my jokes. One of the organizers told me that I was the third-best speaker there, which was oddly specific. But considering who else was speaking at the event, I happily accepted that.

Aside from my time on stage, I spent the majority of the event hanging around the green room so I could rub proverbial elbows with all the other speakers. I even took a few fanboy pictures, dropped a couple of names on social media, and handed out a dozen business cards. It was an eventful trip.

But it wasn't until the last day that it really began to pay off.

It was probably about noon on the final day of the conference when one of the speakers came into the green room in a rush. Dragging her suitcase behind her, she was looking for someone working the event to take her to the airport so she could catch her flight, which was leaving in about two hours or so.

I recognized her from the program. Her name was Laura, and she worked for HubSpot.

Now, if you're not a marketing person, you probably don't know who HubSpot is. Without getting all fancy about it, they develop software for marketing, sales, and customer service. They are very well known within the marketing industry, which isn't terribly relevant here except for the fact that HubSpot also runs the granddaddy of all multimedia conferences, *Inbound*. And *Inbound* was on the list of events where I wanted to speak.

It was the big dream. As far as speaking goes.

Laura found herself a ride to the airport and was about to head for the door before I had a chance to introduce myself. I was already packed up and checked out of the hotel, so I grabbed my stuff and caught up to her before she was able to leave.

"Are you heading to the airport? Do you mind if I hitch a ride with you? My flight is around the same time as yours."

And by "around the same time," I meant that my flight was leaving nowhere near the same time. I had another six or seven hours before I even needed to leave for the airport. But she didn't need to know that.

Laura was all too happy to share her ride with me. We both headed out the door and were handed a gift bag as a thank you for speaking at the event. These things are usually filled with a T-shirt, a pen, and some other swag with the conference logo on it. This one seemed pretty heavy, so we both stuffed ours into our carry-ons and immediately forgot about them.

For the next forty-five minutes, we talked about the conference on our way to the airport. I pretended that I had attended her session when I had really been in the green room the whole time. And she clearly stated that she did not attend mine because she had no idea who I was. The usual speaker thing you do when schmoozing with other speakers on your way to the airport.

I wanted to figure out a way to bring up *Inbound* and see if she could hook me up with an opportunity to speak. But there really was no smooth way of working it into the conversation. So, I kept putting it off. Besides, I had no idea if she even had any input in the decision-making process. Although, that has never stopped me before.

We got to the airport and made our way to the security checkpoint. My window of opportunity was quickly closing. I needed to say something and fast. But before I could, we were waved over to the main security table where both our bags were waiting alongside two security agents.

Apparently, there was something in our bags that had set off the alarms.

They pulled out the two gift bags we had both received for speaking at the event. And inside was a locally sourced bottle of wine that was not allowed through customs without a declaration form.

Laura looked at her watch, looked down at the wine, and then looked at me before saying, "I have about 45 minutes. When does your flight leave?"

"Ummm… I have some time."

It was more like six or seven hours, but who's counting?

"Great! I'll get this open, you go score us some cups, and I'll meet you back here."

And that's what we did.

I headed over to a nearby Starbucks and convinced them to give me two empty venti cups while Laura was working her magic getting the bottles open. We filled each cup to the top, slapped on the lid, did a little cheers, and spent the next thirty minutes or so drinking our wine right outside the security line.

It couldn't have been a more perfect scenario to score an opportunity to speak at *Inbound*. We would bond over some bad local wine at the Halifax airport and then…

"Can you help me get booked to speak at *Inbound*?"

She would give me an emphatic "Yes!"

And then we would high-five or something.

Or at least that's pretty much how the scenario played out in my head. Perhaps I would be a little smoother about it. But you know what I mean. I would make it nearly impossible to say no. Especially given how bad this wine really was.

Just one more sip, and then I'll ask her.

Not yet. Maybe one more sip, and I'll ask her.

Wait. Not yet. Maybe one more sip, and I'll ask her.

This went on for the first five minutes.

And then it hit me.

Here we go again.

This was a pattern that had shown up frequently for me in the past. I would get so focused on "what's next" that I would lose sight of what was happening in the current moment.

Years ago, while I had been on tour with a show, I'd found myself sitting in a dark hotel room. Door closed. Lights out. With nothing but the glow of a computer to illuminate the space in front of me.

If you were to have pulled back the curtains on the opposite side of the room and step through the sliding glass doors hiding behind them, you would have found yourself standing on the balcony staring into the most amazing view of the ocean that you have ever seen.

I was in Miami Beach.

I had been traveling around the country for the better part of a year as the bass player in the Broadway show, *Rent*. One of the most highly acclaimed musicals ever to be performed on stage.

It was my dream gig.

I had dedicated the past fifteen years of my life to perfecting my craft in preparation for the opportunity to perform in a show like this. I had endured thousands of *nos* in order to get to this one *yes*. And yet, while everyone else was either on the beach or exploring the city before the show that night, I had confined myself to a dark hotel room with the curtains drawn. Consumed by a single question.

What's next?

And because I couldn't come up with an immediate answer, I isolated myself from everyone else in the show and missed out on much of the experience.

And that wasn't the only time.

I graduated from college in just three years. Not because I was any smarter or more talented than my fellow classmates. Not even because I worked harder. I graduated one year earlier than everyone else because I was so focused on what was going to come next that I overloaded myself with additional classes in an effort to get out earlier at the expense of enjoying my college years.

And here I was. About to do it again.

I was going to ruin a great time and a great story by trying to sell Laura on the idea of having me speak at a conference instead of simply enjoying the moment.

So, I decided not to ask. And just stayed in the moment instead.

We shared a few more laughs as we finished our wine just in time to get through security. Laura just barely made her flight while I had about another six hours to go before mine. And given the cheap wine headache that I felt coming on, it wasn't going to be a lot of fun.

Later that year, *Inbound* came and went without me on that stage. In fact, I didn't even bother to go. I was pretty disappointed at myself and the fact that I hadn't even tried.

But, as I was about to learn, it ended up working out for the best.

BE FORGIVING

*"Forgiveness is the fragrance that the violet
sheds on the heel that has crushed it."*

— MARK TWAIN

Before we go any further, let's rewind for a second and go back to that little kid with the snap-on cape. Because with each day that passed, as I followed Dick around the neighborhood, I was getting increasingly clear on the actual problem.

You see, I don't know how I defined "changing the world" back then, but I'm pretty sure it included bad guys and explosions. And while I might have outgrown that as I'd gotten older, it had really just morphed into a more adult version of the same thing. Building a school in a third-world country. Or walking from New York to California to raise money for a good cause. Or running into a burning house to save someone I didn't know.

Or something, at the very least, worthy of a made-for-TV movie.

I had set the bar so high that I made it nearly impossible to even see it, let alone reach it. Broadway wasn't enough. Traveling the world wasn't enough. Starting my own successful company wasn't enough. And raising a family wasn't enough.

And I mentally tortured myself on a regular basis because of it. I'm not good enough or I don't deserve it or I'm not worthy. You know. The typical stuff we all have going on inside of our heads.

As I grew older, I became more and more cynical. Convinced that perhaps I was just a naive kid. Or hugged one too many times during my formative years. So, I allowed my purpose of making a difference get overtaken by my need to make a living. After all, it's hard to pay the mortgage on the salary they give you for changing the world. Especially when you aren't very successful at it. So, with a wife, two kids, a mortgage, and a few car payments in tow, I started my company and went to work. Doing stuff. Just like everybody else. Ignoring the thoughts that I was meant for something more. All in the name of a balanced checkbook.

As a result, the years quickly ticked on. Five, ten, fifteen years. Gone. Forgotten. And then I woke up one day and dragged my family to Tampa where I met Dick.

Assuming that you've been paying attention so far, you pretty much know the rest.

And that brings us right back to where we left off.

Over the course of the first year or two in Tampa, I spent a lot of time looking up to Dick as my mentor. Taking note of how he interacted with people and applying those principles to how I showed up for the rest of the world.

Like the time I was about to leave the supermarket when I saw an older couple pushing a cart through the parking lot. Rather than leaving, I jumped out of my car and helped them load their groceries and returned the cart back to the store for them.

Or the time a stray German Shepherd followed Aimee home. He was starving and beat up pretty badly. I took him to the vet to have him checked out, gave him a bath, got him some food, named him Bear, and then helped find him a new home where he is now loved and well taken care of.

Or the time I was kinder or more helpful or more humble or more compassionate or more thoughtful or more generous or more authentic toward some complete stranger than I probably would have been otherwise.

But because of this distorted worldview I had of what it meant to make a difference, there was still something missing. What I was doing didn't matter. Or at least, that was my take on it.

And that's when I got the email.

It showed up one morning in my inbox from a name I didn't recognize. When I opened it, I was greeted by a picture of what appeared to be a car buried in the snow with my name carved on the side of it.

I began to read.

It was from a guy named Seth who had read my blog and had found something about the post that had inspired him to quit his job and move his entire family to a cabin in the mountains. His plan was to dedicate the next few years of his life to the preservation of twenty-five glaciers in Glacier National Park in Montana. He was a professional photographer and dreamed of taking pictures of each of the glaciers in an effort to capture them in a book one last time before they melted and were declassified. And somehow, my blog post had pushed him over the edge, and he'd taken the leap.

Seth created the Glacier Preservation Project in an effort to give the rest of us a chance to experience the beauty of these glaciers one last time before it was too late.

Halfway through his email, he wrote the following.

> *What you are doing does matter. At least to me. What you wrote almost a year and a half ago still rings in my head and encourages me to keep going. I appreciate that you can draw truth out of all the nonsense around and articulate it in a way that I can be able to hold on to at least one clear thought and continue trudging on.*

He went on to talk about the project a little more before he closed his email with:

> *I hope this helps you know that you are changing the world, even if it is only one little seed of wisdom at a time in lots of people's lives. That adds up, you know.*

And the picture? It was not a car buried in the snow. It was a part of the Jackson Glacier. One of the glaciers that were at risk. He had written my name in the snow with his finger in order to immortalize (his words, not mine) my involvement in this life-altering project.

I was speechless. Again.

That doesn't happen very often, let alone twice in one book.

After reading it a few times, I forwarded it to my wife with the following message.

Someone who had been reading my blog sent me this in response to one of my posts. This is what I want to wake up to every day. I don't care what it pays.

It was the same feeling that had me running home from my high school jazz band concert at the senior center.

That email from Seth and the picture of my name in the glacier were physical proof beyond the shadow of a doubt how blind I was to the difference I was already making by the little things I was doing on a daily basis.

Just like Dick.

Even though I never built a school in a third world country. Or walked from New York to California to raise money for a good cause. Or ran into a burning house to save someone I didn't know.

It was the first time I was able to step back and acknowledge myself for having done something truly extraordinary. It was also the first time I realized how critical I was of myself; all the times that I had made an impact on someone or something but was too busy beating myself up to realize it.

It was a devastating moment. Years of abuse. All by my own hand.

It would have been easy to dip back into my old playlist. Remind myself that I probably didn't deserve it. Or that I wasn't good enough. Or that I wasn't worthy. But instead, I decided to forgive myself. For all of it.

For not saving the world at six years old. And for the unrealistic expectations I had every day thereafter. For not stopping long enough to acknowledge the good. And for allowing my failures to define who I was. For not being the husband I could have been. And for falling short of being the father I should have been. For every time I saw someone who needed help and did nothing. And for every time I saw someone who needed help and did something but didn't acknowledge myself for it.

I needed to forgive myself for not taking better care of that six-year-old kid with the snaps on his pajamas who wanted nothing more than to simply change the world.

So, that's what I did. I forgave myself.

And it was a good thing that I did. Because there was just no way I was going to be able to take on what was about to come next without having let go of all of that stuff first.

BE GRATEFUL

*"There is no future. There is no past. I live
this moment as my last."*

— JONATHAN LARSON

It all started with an email. I probably wrote a dozen different versions before I got it right. One version was too long. Another was too impersonal. One version sounded too desperate. Another sounded too indifferent. Eventually, I landed on what I thought was the perfect mix of personal, fun, and to the point with a dash of desperation.

> *Question for you... Is there ANNNNNNNYYYY
> way that you can hook me up with a little love at
> Inbound so I can possibly speak? Any stage, any
> session. Doesn't matter.*

It had been a year since Laura and I shared a bottle of cheap local wine at the Halifax airport and I was hoping and praying that she remembered me.

I was not about to have another repeat of the previous year. *Inbound* wasn't scheduled for a few months, but this time, I was committed to speaking at the event. I was ready to share my story about Dick on a bigger stage, and I couldn't think of a bigger platform than *Inbound*.

Eighteen minutes after sending that email, Laura responded by asking me if I would like to do what was called a "Bold Talk." It was *Inbound*'s version of a TED-style talk where you have twelve minutes to share a bold new idea with the audience.

I'll take it!

I named my talk "Be a Dick," which the powers that be at *Inbound* almost immediately insisted be changed to "Be a D*ck." Not to be confused with "Be a Duck," which could have been equally entertaining, I suppose.

But none of that mattered. This was it! I was speaking at *Inbound*! It had been a dream of mine for years, and it was actually going to happen.

Over the course of the next few months, I practiced telling the story about Dick and each of the principles I had learned along the way. I would practice at home. I would practice in the car. I would practice while riding my bike. And ultimately, when I found myself in Boston for the conference, I practiced in public every day as I walked between the venue and my hotel.

By the time the day came when I would have to tell my story, I had already run through it hundreds of times. I had been on that stage hundreds of times. I had said the words hundreds of times. I saw the standing ovation hundreds of times.

And yet, I was still nervous.

There were two other speakers and one emcee presenting in the same room as me. The other speakers were

Mark Schaefer and Tamsen Webster, and the emcee was Christopher Penn. If you aren't active in the world of marketing, these names probably don't mean much to you. Sorry, guys. But let me just say that they are true powerhouses in their own right. "Brilliant" would be the only way to describe them. How I'd been put in the same room with them was beyond me.

The room began to fill up quickly. I saw a lot of people I knew from my online community, like C.C. Chapman and Joel Comm. Both of whom were "internet celebrities" in this space. At least in my mind.

Once the room had filled to capacity, they closed the doors and stood guard to make sure nobody else entered during our session. Looking around, I saw that every seat was taken, and many people were standing along the back wall. We had officially reached standing-room-only status.

Mark Schaefer was scheduled to speak first. Imagine how I felt when Chris announced that the first speaker would be Mark—then paused for what felt like three hours while I had a panic attack—Schaeffer. Whew! That was a close one. I was scheduled to speak second, followed by Tamsen.

Mark told a very personal story about depression. And I was supposed to follow that up with a talk about Dick. It's almost as if somebody is out to get me sometimes. Anyway, five minutes before he finished, I was waved over to the soundboard where they clipped this ridiculously giant Lavalier microphone to my white shirt. And then the only thing left to do was wait by the side of the stage for Chris to introduce me.

"Ladies and gentlemen, please welcome Marc Ensign!"

I couldn't hear or see anything as all five of my senses began to shut down due to nerves.

I walked onto the stage without tripping and thanked Chris as I shook his hand. So far, so good. I stopped in the middle of the stage and paused as I looked out into the audience. I took a deep breath and started with the exact same words I used to open this book.

"My name is Marc. And I am a Dick.

"I'm a Dick to all of my friends. And to my family. I'm a Dick to people I know. And to people I don't know.

"In fact, if we were to bump into each other someday, whether it be online or in real life, I would probably be a Dick to you, too.

"It's nothing personal. It's just who I am."

The rest was a bit of a blur until the very end when I grabbed the baseball off of the podium and was immediately transported back to that moment when Dick was standing in my doorway the day he had given it to me.

"This is who I want to be."

At first, I didn't even realize that I'd said it. I had forgotten what I was supposed to say and instead went right back to that moment, and in a split second, the past year and a half had literally flashed before my eyes.

I was doing everything I could to fight back the tears as it all came back to me in one sudden flood of emotion. The last few minutes of my talk were completely improvised as I dipped in and out of awareness, doing everything I could to remain present on stage.

I thanked the audience, walked back down the steps, and took my seat while they announced Tamsen to the stage. My phone was blowing up on all of the various social media channels, since everyone in the room was sharing their new experience of my neighbor, Dick.

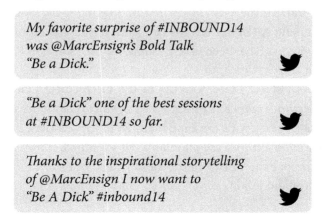

My favorite surprise of #INBOUND14 was @MarcEnsign's Bold Talk "Be a Dick."

"Be a Dick" one of the best sessions at #INBOUND14 so far.

Thanks to the inspirational storytelling of @MarcEnsign I now want to "Be A Dick" #inbound14

That kind of thing does wonders for your ego, by the way.

After Tamsen was done speaking, I stuck around the room for thirty minutes or so talking to audience members and hearing stories about all of the Dicks in their lives. But as much as I loved the attention, I was doing everything I could to leave so I could get back to my hotel room.

They eventually threw us all out to reset the room for the next group of speakers, and I left the conference center and walked to my hotel, where I went up to my room and closed the door behind me.

And I cried.

I have never told anyone that before. Not even my wife. You're pretty much the first one to know.

I didn't cry because I made it through the talk. Or because there were a lot of people in the room. Or because it was well received. Or because it might do something to boost my career.

I cried because, for the first time in my life, I was so grateful for everything that had brought me to this moment. All of it. Even the bad stuff. Because without it, I wouldn't have been able to stand on that stage and tell that story.

As I stood there, looking in the mirror of my hotel room with tears streaming down my face, I saw that six-year-old boy with the cape snapped to his pajamas. Preparing to jump on the ottoman as he screamed, "I'm going to change the world," and I couldn't help but smile.

You did it, kid.

BE VULNERABLE

"To share your weakness is to make yourself vulnerable; to make yourself vulnerable is to show your strength."

—Criss Jami

There is one thing I forgot to mention in all of this. It's actually pretty important to the whole story. I guess I should have said something sooner, but it never really came up.

Dick had no idea any of this was going on.

That's right. I'd never told him about it.

Now, before you give me a hard time, you should know that I tried. I went out to dinner with him so I could talk to him about it. I invited him out for ice cream so I could talk to him about it. I took Cali out for several unnecessary walks so I could talk to him about it. But as much as I wanted to, I couldn't drum up the courage to say anything.

So, I didn't.

I guess I was terrified that he would hate the idea. Or worse. That he would hate me for it. I didn't want him to think I was making fun of his name. Or using our relationship as a way to cash in. Or stalking him to the point where he might feel uncomfortable walking around the neighborhood. None of that was true, but I could see why he might have thought it was. So, I never said anything. I just quietly rode the wave for a while until one day, it was too late, and he found out on his own.

It wasn't until a few months after *Inbound* that I was sent a link to the video of my talk. I couldn't have been more excited. Outside of the blog post, I hadn't really shared too much about the story other than to my close friends and relatives. So, this was my chance to share with my community. And that's what I did. Without giving it much thought, I shared the video on Facebook. And guess who clicked the "Like" button.

Yup. Dick.

As soon as I saw that, I panicked. I shut off the computer and hid under the bed. Afraid of whatever repercussions would come with it. I had been successfully hiding this from him for over a year and a half while we walked our dogs around the neighborhood. While he invited me into his home. While we went out for ice cream. While we got our families together. It was as if I had been leading a double life. And it was too late to turn back now.

But he didn't say anything about it. At least, not at the time.

A few weeks later, we made dinner plans with Dick and Rita for Aimee's birthday. They decided to pick us up since they had chosen the restaurant and we had no idea how to get there. It was way out in the middle of nowhere. That's all we knew about it. When we got to the car, I noticed that Rita was in the back seat, so Aimee got in the back with her while I climbed into the passenger seat.

The whole thing felt a bit like a mob hit.

We left the house, and while the girls were in the back talking, Dick finally broke the tension I was feeling.

"I saw the video of the talk you gave. What's that all about?"

Awkward silence.

"Dick, I want you to know that I didn't mean anything bad by it. I had written a blog post a while ago and had a chance to speak at this conference and…"

Blah. Blah. Blah.

I rambled for a few minutes. Making a bunch of excuses that made little to no sense.

And then I stopped and let my guard down, got vulnerable, and told him the truth. I told him where I had been a year-and-a-half earlier, how much I had been struggling, and how I had felt lost. I told him how I questioned whether my life really mattered or made a difference. And then I told him how meeting him on that walk with my kids when we'd first moved to the neighborhood had changed my life. That it had forced me to see things differently. And that I was a better person today than I had been before we'd met. Because of him.

I told him everything. And it felt good to get it out of my system. I had been waiting a long time to say all of that. And regardless of how he responded, I felt at peace.

And then he finally broke the silence. "If you think you can help some people with our story, I think it's great."

And that was it. I had his blessing.

We spent the next thirty minutes or so driving to the restaurant. And while I sat in that car, I couldn't help but reflect on everything that had happened over the course of the past year and a half.

It felt good to tell the story on my blog and watch the traffic shut my website down. And it felt good to get emails from people from all over the world telling me about the "Dicks" in their lives. And it felt good to share the story in front of a room full of my marketing heroes and have a crowd of people waiting to talk to me when I was done. But none of that compared to how good it felt to finally tell that story to the one person who needed to hear it the most.

Dick.

BE AMBITIOUS

*"I arise in the morning torn between a
desire to save the world and a desire to savor
the world."*

— E. B. WHITE

As the next year or two passed, I continued to instill
these principles in my life. Eventually, I found that I was
becoming more and more unfulfilled with the time I was
spending in my marketing agency. We were doing fine.
But there was something missing.

So, I left.

I resigned from my own company and walked away
with the hopes of starting something new that would
allow me to serve people on a bigger scale. Something
that would allow me to make a bigger difference. My goal
was to take everything I had learned from my past and
start an agency that would help people discover their
message and get it in front of the world.

The only challenge was finding the right name.

Now, if you have ever tried to name a company, you know the living hell that process can be. After a month or two of banging my head against the wall, I was handed an ultimatum from my wife. "Pick a name by the end of the weekend, or I will pick one for you." Remember how I told you that Aimee wasn't very good at decorating? Well, she's equally bad at picking the names of companies. So, I had a lot of incentive to pick something. Even if it wasn't very good.

I began feverishly writing down names. Most of which were pretty bad. Like Liquid Frog. That was one of them. I swear. The logo was going to be a frog crawling out of a blender. Not my best idea. But hey, it was certainly memorable.

Somewhere in all of this, the name LoudMouse came up, and I instantly fell in love with it. It represented everything I stood for. This idea of giving anyone a big voice, no matter how small they may be.

My head was spinning with all the things I could do with it to grab attention, like making business cards out of mousetraps. It was a horrible idea that could have very easily ended with someone getting hurt and me being the recipient of a lawsuit. So, the mousetraps were out. But I had plenty of other ideas that wouldn't result in someone losing a finger.

There was just one problem.

The domain LoudMouse.com was already taken.

Not one to quit right away, I reached out to the owner of LoudMouse.com, thinking I could perhaps buy the domain since there was no active website up at the time.

A few days later, I got a call back from Lance.

Lance owned the domain. And, as it turned out, I was not the first person interested in buying it from him. In fact, by the looks of things, I was going to have to cash in my kids' college fund if I wanted it. He had received previous offers of four and five figures for the domain but had turned them all down.

I was about to hang up, knowing there was no way I was going to spend that much for the domain name, when the call took a bizarre turn.

He began to tell me that after receiving my email, he'd followed the link in my signature to my blog and had landed on my post about Dick. Something about it struck a nerve with him, and without hesitation, he decided to give me the domain name. For free. No strings attached.

Lance was a Dick.

He transferred the domain name that night, and Loud-Mouse was born. I didn't have a logo. Or a clear direction. Or a website. Or any prospective clients.

All I had was a domain name and the blind faith of a complete stranger who believed in me more than I believed in myself. You see, I wasn't willing to spend the money on the domain name. Yet Lance was willing to give up the money for me to have it.

To this day, that is something that continues to drive me forward. That there was someone out there who believed in me more than I believed in myself. And I work really hard every day to make up for that.

But here's the really cool thing about it.

In business, there is so much talk about measuring the return on investment with everything you do. If you pay for an ad, you measure how much the ad cost versus how much new business it brought in. Or if you hire a new employee, you measure how much their salary is versus how much work gets done and the value of the results.

But we never measure many of the things that actually matter. Like being kind or being helpful or being generous. Probably because those are almost impossible to measure. Yet if I have learned nothing else throughout all of this, I've learned that living these principles was the best investment I ever made.

In the years that followed, I put a lot of effort into challenging myself with each of these principles. Sometimes, I succeeded and it brought something incredibly valuable into my life. Other times, I failed miserably and it brought something equally valuable into my life.

But in the end, I have never regretted applying these principles to my friends, my family, my clients, my team, or even complete strangers.

Like I said earlier. It's nothing personal. It's just who I am.

A Dick.

CONCLUSION

"Art is never finished, only abandoned."

— Leonardo da Vinci

It's been a lifetime since I took that first walk with the kids when we met Dick. Or at least it feels as though it has been. And a lot has happened since.

Believe it or not, Bella is now seventeen years old and Zach is twelve. I won't tell you how old Aimee is because I'd really like to live to see tomorrow.

The other night, we were watching a program on Apple TV+ called *Dear...* with Lin Manuel Miranda, the writer of *Hamilton*. He's a family favorite of ours. While Lin (that's what his friends call him) was talking about writing *Hamilton* over the course of seven years, he described it as a tap on his shoulder that wouldn't leave him alone. He would pick it up for a while and then get distracted by something else, and then, sure enough, it would come back and tap him on the shoulder again.

And this continued until he actually created the show.

That has been my experience writing this book. Except maybe without all of the singing and dancing.

In the years since meeting Dick, I wrote this book seventeen different times. That is not a joke or an exaggeration.

And each time, I threw it out because it wasn't quite right.

I mostly blamed perfectionism. Thinking that I wasn't willing to release it until it was perfect. But that wasn't it. It's not perfect now, and yet you are holding it and reading it. I wasn't willing to release it because it wasn't right. One version was too dark. Another was too preachy. And one version actually included step-by-step instructions on how to be a Dick, which made it impossible to read without rolling your eyes.

A lot of people knew I was writing the book at the time and felt let down when it didn't come out. Some lost faith in me. While others made sure to remind me that I had failed. Some encouraged me to release what I had and move on. While others recommended that I walk away from it.

But as much as I wanted to close this chapter of my life and move on, this book kept showing back up…

Tap. Tap. Tap.

Tapping me on the shoulder again.

So, I would get back to work. Write the book over the course of a few more months. And then throw it away all over again. And this went on for the better part of five or six years. Altogether, I wrote roughly 350,000 words. Every single one of which was thrown out. Until recently.

Tap. Tap. Tap.

I hadn't looked at it for over a year, yet it was back.

I opened a blank document and began to type. Only this time, something was different. I don't know if it was because I saw it through a different pair of eyes or because I had changed so much over the previous year, but I was writing a much different book. I ended up writing the entire book in eight days. The one you are reading right now. And throughout the course of those eight days, I found it almost impossible to step away.

In that same episode of *Dear...*, Lin Manuel Miranda said something that captured how I felt while writing this book for the eighteenth time.

"So much of writing is just about meeting the moment as honestly as possible."

I believe that to be true in the writing of this book. And I believe that this was the right moment. And this was the right book.

And that brings me to the end of my story, but the beginning of yours.

Now, in case you haven't figured it out yet, this story was never about me. It was never about Dick, either. It was always about you.

I firmly believe that we all want to change the world in our own little way, but we get stuck due to the misconception that we must build a school in a third-world nation or walk across the country to raise money for a cause or rush into a burning house and save someone. Or whatever you set for yourself as a gauge of doing something that matters.

But that's not how it works.

And that is really the point of this whole story and what I learned from Dick. To show you how easy it is to change the world. In fact, it's so easy that you don't need a step-by-step process to learn how to be kind. You already have everything you need within you. It's now just a matter of doing something with it.

This stuff isn't hard. And it doesn't require step-by-step instructions. You don't need to take a course. And you don't need to ask permission.

Here is all you have to do if you want to be a Dick.

The next time you are walking down the street and run into someone new, I want you to remember this story and choose to be kinder. Or more helpful. Or more humble. The next time you are talking to one of your kids, I want you to remember this story and be more compassionate. Or more thoughtful. Or more present. The next time you are at the store and you see someone struggling, I want you to remember this story and be more thoughtful. Or more generous. Or more grateful.

Because being a Dick is how you really change the world.

JOIN THE MOVEMENT

We need more people like Dick in this world. Especially now. And that's where you come in.

Sure, you could read this book and then move on to the next one. See it as nothing more than a good story with a prepubescent joke as a twist. Or you can do something about it.

I would like to challenge you to do something about it.

Join us. Be a Dick. And when you do, I want to hear about it. Here are a few ways you can get involved:

> *If you have a story about someone you know who is a Dick, you can share it by going to IWantToBeADick.com and tell me all about them! I may even feature your story on the website!*

> *If you have a quick Dick sighting that you want to share on social media, use the hashtag #BeADick and let me know about it!*

Or you can just be a Dick. After all, the world needs you. Don't let us down. Maybe the next book will be about you.....

ACKNOWLEDGMENTS

I know that this is usually the part of the book where you stop reading and head toward the last page so you can leave a five-star review (hint, hint). That is, of course, unless there is a chance that your name might be mentioned.

Please let this time be different. This time, read through the acknowledgments. You may not know all of the people on this list, but I bet you know a few. And besides, whether you know them or not, I'm sure they would really want you to see their name in print. After all, each person here is responsible for helping me extract this book from the now lifeless and exhausted puddle that was once my brain. The least you could do is read it. You've come this far, right?

To my wife Aimee and my kids Bella and Zach. All of this is for you. Every single word. The weekends spent at Barnes & Noble. The after-dinner walks that I missed. The noise-canceling headphones. The locked doors. The times when I was a dick when I should have been a Dick. The hours hiding in the bathroom. Every time I said I would be done in a few minutes only to have you fall asleep hours later when I lost track of time. That faraway look in my eye as I was supposed to be listening but instead was working through something in my head. I know that writing this book was harder for you than it was for me, and I want to thank you with everything I have for your love, support, and patience.

To my friend, my mentor, and my neighbor Dick. This book would not have been possible without you. I can't express how much love, respect, and appreciation I have for you. So much would be different in my life, had we not bumped into each other that day. And for that, I am eternally grateful.

To Rita and the rest of Dick's family. We are some of the luckiest people on this planet for having started our new life here down the street from you. Thank you for welcoming us with such open arms.

To my Mom, who, ironically enough, is named Jane (get it?). You gave me the vision to see the story and the heart to be able to tell it. Both of which made this book possible.

To my Dad, who overcame more than anyone could ask in order for me to be able to be the husband and father I am today.

To my sister Rachel for being born… to be alive. (That's a private joke. Don't try to figure out what that means. It's really stupid and involves sock puppets. I'm not kidding.)

To Chris Brogan for your friendship, inspiration, support, and, of course, for writing the foreword. I can't tell you what it meant to have you write the first few words of this book. It has been an honor to know you over the years and to call you my friend. This book could have easily been called *Be a Chris*, but it wouldn't have sold as many copies. Maybe next time.

To my friend and coach (or whatever the heck you like to be called) Chris Delaney for seeing who I was beyond all of that crusty stuff on the outside. The Dick has been released. Thanks for the push.

To Jeni Larson Hott, one of my favorite people in the whole wide world. You are such an inspiration to me on so many levels. Every time I started to feel myself fall apart during this process, you were there to talk me off the ledge. To remind me of how important this message was. I probably would have given up long ago if it had not been for many of your pep talks.

To Laura Fitton for sticking your neck out and saying *yes* to some complete nobody who wanted to show up to one of the biggest conferences on the planet and talk about being a Dick. Or, technically being a D*ck. You have no idea what an honor that was for me. I still pinch myself every now and again.

To Joel Comm and C.C. Chapman. You were both there to hear me tell this story the first time to actual people at *Inbound*. And you both made it a point to tell me how much you loved it. Whether you meant it or not and whether you knew it or not, those words legitimized everything I was working on and helped set me on the course I am currently walking.

To Tamsen Webster for being so amazing that people filled that room to see you, and you still pretended like they were there to see me. You helped me wrap my arms around this giant story, and for that, I am grateful.

To my friend Lee Silverstein. For seven years, I told you I would write this book, and it never happened. A lot of people lost faith in me during that time. You were not one of them, and I love you for that.

To Wil Wheaton, who thinks that being a dick is a bad thing. Except in this case. You shut down my server three times by sharing the original post I wrote about Dick. It was the first time I realized I was on to something big. In a strange way, I owe you one for that! Speaking of which, if you could share the book as well, it would really help!

To Hal Elrod for always being a good friend and allowing me to watch your journey from the front row.

To Kevin "The Hammer" Sullivan for showing me the lighter side of life and being one of the funniest people I know.

To Gonzalo Paternoster for always listening. Even when I give you really bad advice that may or may not have ruined your speaking career before it even started.

To Karen Rowe for not giving up on me, even though I have asked you to edit this on several occasions only to disappear for years at a time.

Additional thanks to everyone who played a role in this story, whether you knew it or not. Matthew McGouran, Kevin McGouran, Stephen Lowe, Phyllis Lowe, Larry Lowe, Phil Gerbyshak, Lisa Demmi, Mark Traphagen, Les Dossey, Peg Fitzpatrick, Sue B. Zimmerman, Anthony Amos, Vinnie Fischer, Lisa Haen, Shane Mahoney, Scott Lesnick, Nate Lindquist, Margaret Wright, Stephanie Mack, Lance McCollough, Topher Morrison, Kelly Oliver, Bill Renna, Stan Padgett, Brad Spencer, John Pink, John Policastro, Jairek and Amanda Robbins, Jonathan Larson, Mia Voss, Kathy Klotz-Guest, Bryan Kramer, Mike Ganino, Ron Collier, Brianna Deleasa, Mike Calhoun,

Chris Jenkins, Delatorro L. McNeal II, Colleen Hare Sweeney, David Glickman, John Tigh, Dominic Lacquaniti, Viveka von Rosen-Martin, and the countless others who have come in and out of my life over the years.

To all of those who have inspired me to be a better person who are not named Dick but instead are named Gary Vaynerchuk, Chris Guillebeau, Michael Hyatt, Jeff Goins, Tony Robbins, Jay Baer, Donald Miller, Ann Handley, Darren Hardy, Stephen Covey, David Meerman Scott, Julian Smith, Seth Godin, Ray Dalio, Guy Kawasaki, Simon Sinek, Malcom Gladwell, Mark Schaefer, Jon Acuff, Tim Ferriss, and Scott Stratten.

And, of course, to you reading this right now. Regardless of who you are or where you are. If you ever need a ladder, please let me know.

I have two.

ABOUT THE AUTHOR

Marc Ensign

Marc Ensign's story began when he was a kid who wanted to change the world. Upon realizing that it might take a little longer than anticipated, he got sidetracked and found himself playing bass on Broadway with the Tony Award-winning show *Rent*. He was completely unqualified (his words) but had a gift for marketing himself, and the rest is Broadway history.

Fast-forward a bunch of years, and Marc is now "The Big Cheese" at LoudMouse, a branding and digital marketing agency specializing in making some of the world's most inspiring people and organizations impossible to ignore. Visit MarcEnsign.com or LoudMouse.com to see what else he's up to.

Dick

Dick is Marc's neighbor and friend.

9 781649 994677